SMALL BUSINESS PROCUREMENT

K Hughes

Copyright © 2016 Kay Hughes

All rights reserved.

ISBN: 978-1537353258

ISBN-13: 153735325X

Chris and Michelle

Thank You!

FORWARD

The mantra for this book is Clear, Concise and Uncomplicated which gives you an idea of what to expect as you read through this short book. Within the context of this book, Entrepreneurs and Start-Ups are also included whenever Small Businesses are mentioned. Every company started with an Entrepreneur who had an idea, became a Start-Up and then grew into a Small Business. This book is dedicated to Small Businesses; however, you, your spouse or your best buddy or someone you just hired may be the entire "Procurement Department". No worries! All companies have to start somewhere and you are admired for taking the risk to realize a vision. Follow this book in setting up good Procurement policies and processes and you'll do fine whether you're a $20,000 or $20,000,000 Small Business.

I almost forgot the legal stuff...this book does not refer to any known person or company. In fact, the Martian Menagerie Company used in the examples in this book was incorporated on Mars and is entirely fictional...at this time.

CONTENTS

Part I – Procurement Defined   1
- Procurement Defined
- How To Structure a Procurement Department
- The Three Fundamental Tenets of Procurement
- Initial Setup of a Procurement Department
- Categories and Commodities
- Procurement Personnel
- How to Hire the Right People

Part II – Procurement Policies & Processes 25
- Procurement Policies
- Contracts
- Contract Structure
- Signing the Contract
- Contract Management
- Vendor Questionnaire

Part III – Strategic Sourcing & RFP   59
- Strategic Sourcing
- Request for Proposal (RFP)
- RFP Summary
- RFP Step 1 – Identify the RFP Team Members
- RFP Step 2 – Define the Scope of the RFP
- RFP Step 3 – Identify RFP Vendors
- RFP Step 4 – Prepare the RFP Vendor Packet
- RFP Step 5 – Review & Score Vendor Proposals
- RFP Step 6 – Vendor Presentations & Awards
- RFP Step 7 – Transition to New Vendors

Part IV – Reporting, Negotiations and How to Work With a Large Corporation   **87**
- Reporting
- Negotiations
- How to Work With a Large Corporation
- 10 Iron Clad Rules for Small Businesses

PART I

PROCUREMENT DEFINED

PART

PROCUREMENT SERVICE

PROCUREMENT DEFINED

What exactly is Procurement? A dictionary will give a very narrow definition of Procurement pertaining to the word itself. Ask people in Procurement at a large U.S. corporation and they will describe their role as Strategic Sourcing or Supply Chain or Contract Preparation or Vendor Management. A person in Procurement at a Start-Up or a Small Business will say they do "everything". Here, however, the focus is on Small Businesses so we will focus on "everything".

Under the mandate of Clear, Concise and Uncomplicated, here is the definition of Procurement:

"Procurement is the strategic sourcing and management of vendors in order to control costs and mitigate risk."

HOW TO STRUCTURE A PROCUREMENT DEPARTMENT

THE THREE FUNDAMENTAL TENETS OF PROCUREMENT

It is a common misconception that Procurement controls how and where the company's money is spent. Budgets and how the money is spent belongs under the direct control of the various Business Units (BUs) or Lines of Business (LOBs). Procurement advises, presents options, prepares detailed analytical data and makes recommendations to the BUs so that they can make informed and rational decisions on how and where to spend their budgeted money. Procurement does not show favoritism to any department and is focused solely on doing what's best for the company as a whole.

Procurement is made up of three fundamental tenets: *Supply Chain, Legal and Finance*.

Procurement balances need, risk and cost on behalf of the entire company. Supply Chain focuses on manufacturing the product; Legal concentrates on mitigation of risk; and Finance controls the flow of money. It is Procurement's job to view all of these functions from a holistic and unbiased point of view for the benefit of the entire company.

In many cases, one or more of these departments is so narrowly focused and has the loudest voice that it influences how the company is run. It is often said that

Supply Chain grabs all the attention, Legal slows the business, and Finance has a death grip on the money. Procurement is typically caught between all of these fractious departments but a good Procurement department can diffuse these situations and bring cohesion and logic to bear.

Let's take an in-depth look at the three fundamental tenets that Procurement is based upon:

SUPPLY CHAIN

Supply Chain is the sourcing, receipt, production, and delivery of products or services critical to the business. The concept of Supply Chain is not complicated: Each point of movement from one step to the next is a link in the Supply Chain. The longer and more complicated the Supply Chain, the easier it is to break a link in the chain. It is Procurement's job to make sure there are no breaks in the Supply Chain by working with the BU to strategically source new vendors and develop strong vendor relationships. Procurement is also involved in inventory management, stocking agreements, and the penalty phase when vendors drop the ball and don't deliver the goods or services as promised.

LEGAL

Procurement works very closely with the company's legal counsel to mitigate risk by developing the language used in vendor contracts. A good legal department will have a variety of contract templates developed in conjunction with Procurement to address most normal vendor agreements. In addition, Legal works closely with Procurement to develop contract policies and procedures so that both departments are not overwhelmed with non-critical vendor agreements.

FINANCE

Procurement works closely with the Treasury and Finance departments to set up the processes by which the vendors invoice and the company pays for the goods and services purchased. Within the context of this book, both Treasury and Finance will be referred to as Finance.

INITIAL SETUP OF A PROCUREMENT DEPARTMENT

A Procurement department is typically split into two divisions: Direct and Indirect. These two divisions may also be known as Costs of Goods Sold (COGS) and Non-COGS or Addressable and Non-Addressable.

DIRECT & INDIRECT

DIRECT is all of the products directly used in the manufacture of the goods.

INDIRECT is everything else.

COGS & NON-COGS

COGS are all of the products directly used in the manufacture of the goods including labor costs.

NON-COGS is everything else.

ADDRESSABLE & NON-ADDRESSABLE

ADDRESSABLE is all spend which can be influenced by Procurement.

NON-ADDRESSABLE is all spend which cannot be influenced by Procurement (Ex.: Taxes, State Fees, Permits, etc.).

In order to keep with the mandate of Clear, Concise and Uncomplicated Procurement, we will focus on Direct and Indirect in this book. This is the most common split of categories within Procurement departments.

Let's visit Mars and the Martian Menagerie Company to see how they identified the Direct and Indirect products and services.

MARTIAN MENAGERIE COMPANY

The Martian Menagerie Company manufactures cages for all types of animals found on Mars. From the smallest mouse-like creature called the Mini-Mars Button Mouse to the largest elephant-sized Mega Mars Marsupial, the Martian Menagerie Company has a cage that works for all its customers throughout the galaxy. Rated for inter-planetary travel, each cage comes with different options including the award winning fur-lined cage for the Soft-Shelled Pigometer.

Let's take a look at how the Martian Menagerie Company has set up their Procurement department.

DIRECT PRODUCTS

Each cage is manufactured using a Bill Of Materials (BOM). Every part, screw, food bowl and piece of material is considered a Direct product because it is the sum of all parts that are used in manufacturing products shipped to the customer. An easy way to remember how to classify products as "Direct" is to add "to the Customer" at the end of "Direct". If the customer doesn't receive it, then it is not considered "Direct".

DIRECT BOM

Raw Steel

Finished Steel

Nuts, Bolts & Screws

Clasps, Hinges & Pins

Locks

Food

Food Bowls

Food Bowl Accessories (spoons, scoops, etc.)

Water Containers

Cage Padding & Covers

Grooming Tools

INDIRECT PRODUCTS & SERVICES

Everything that isn't a Direct Product goes into the Indirect category. Below are some of the products and services considered Indirect. This is not a comprehensive list by any means but it will give the Small Business owner an idea of what is considered Indirect. In the olden days on Mars when Martian Mega-Dinosaurs swam in the "canals", Indirect was called Administrative Services or Overhead.

Office Supplies

Janitorial Services

Software Licenses

Legal Fees

Building Maintenance

Coffee

Travel

Warehouse Rental

Energy

Landscaping

Temporary Labor

Health Care

Payroll

INDIRECT SERVICES

As part of their direct facing Customer offerings, the Martian Menagerie Company also offers the following Cage Services: Cage Cleaning, Cage Pick-up and Drop-Off, and Cage Refurbishment. These are all revenue generating activities and direct to the Customer. These Services should be considered Direct because the supplies used to clean the cages and the materials used to refurbish the cage would be categorized as BOM as part of the services. In addition, the Martin Menagerie Company sells the cleaning supplies direct to the customers as a revenue generating Line of Business (LOB). Labor costs should also be considered part of the Indirect Services because it is part of the services directly provided to the customer.

CATEGORIES & COMMODITIES

Procurement personnel manage Categories and Commodities. Commodities are the individual products and Categories are made up of a number of Commodities. It is recommended that Procurement personnel switch categories or commodities every three to five years to get fresh eyes and points of view on the contracts, negotiations and vendor setups. The movement of Categories and Commodities provides cross-training and also breaks any vendor relationships with Procurement personnel that have grown too close or too complacent.

Let's visit to the Martian Menagerie Company to see how they set up their Direct and Indirect categories:

DIRECT CATEGORIES

The Martian Menagerie Company has set up two Direct Categories made up of different commodities for its cages:

CAGE	CAGE ACCESSORIES
Raw Steel	Food
Finished Steel	Bowls & Accessories
Nuts, Bolts & Screws	Water Containers
Clasps, Hinges & Pins	Cage Padding & Covers
Locks	Grooming Tools

The Cage category is made up of non-perishable products that form a complete product. There is a fixed set of materials for the Cages that do not decay and inventory can be managed in a predictable fashion.

Good inventory management skills are needed for this category but it is an easy category to manage with no complexity. This Category would be managed by a Category Manager or even a Commodity Manager since the main components are made of metal and could be categorized as one Commodity.

The Cage Accessories category is a more complex Category and, therefore, would be the most difficult to manage. Complexity is created in this category by the reliance on weather, availability, quality, delivery and shelf life of the food. There is also complexity managing the accompanying Bowls & Accessories, Water Containers, Cage Padding & Covers, and Grooming Tools. Each product varies in accordance to the size and type of cage and its occupant which requires advanced inventory management skills. This Category would be managed by a Senior Category Manager.

INDIRECT CATEGORIES

The Martian Menagerie Company has split its Indirect Categories into two Categories:

CATEGORY ONE	CATEGORY TWO
OpEx	CapEx
Office Supplies & Machines	Energy
Coffee	IT
Janitorial Services	Legal Fees
Building Maintenance	Purchasing Cards
Landscaping	Travel
Warehouse Rental	Temporary Labor

These categories were split by complexity with the Senior Category Manager overseeing Indirect Category Two. Notice that CapEx and OpEx have been added to these categories.

Let's talk a moment about...

CAPEX & OPEX

Capital Expenditures (CapEx) and Operating Expenses (OpEx) are two different streams of spending within a company. A CapEx designation is assigned by Finance to products that are usually permanent fixtures, meet a certain dollar threshold and are depreciable in nature. OpEx are the day-to-day expenses used in running the company. For example, the machine used to bend the steel for the cages would be designated as CapEx because it meets the dollar threshold, is permanent and can be depreciated. The electricity used to run the machine would be considered OpEx because electricity does not meet the criteria for Capex. Each company has a different interpretation of CapEx triggered by different criteria set forth by the Finance Department. No matter how it is designated, the designation itself is never done by Procurement; only Finance can make the determination of whether an item is CapEx or OpEx.

Author's Note: It is my sincere belief that Finance has a coin with one side saying CapEx and the other side OpEx. When the designation is not clear, the coin is tossed and a designation assigned. I'm sure I'll catch flack for that statement!

PROCUREMENT PERSONNEL

Now that we've established the definitions of Commodities and Categories, let's focus on Procurement personnel, their roles, and their responsibilities. Usually, Procurement reports up through Finance or Supply Chain; however, this is not a good idea. If Procurement reports to either Supply Chain or Finance, it is unable to remain unbiased because of the reporting hierarchy. Procurement should always be a stand-alone division within a company reporting directly to the President.

By the way, there is no right or wrong number of people in a Procurement department. The number of individuals can, and should, fluctuate as business needs dictate. It is the type of people, their expertise and experience that will determine the success of a Procurement department for your Small Business.

Keeping with the mandate of Clear, Concise and Uncomplicated, these are the most commonly used titles and job descriptions currently used in both small and large companies:

Vice President or Procurement Director (Working) – Responsible for the overall leadership and management of Procurement personnel and the assignment of Categories and Commodities. The Vice President or Procurement Director is a member of the Leadership Team and builds interdepartmental relationships; supervises personnel; prepares presentations; develops reports, policies and procedures; trains personnel; and is responsible for the performance of the Procurement department. Highly strategic categories and commodities are managed by the Vice President or Procurement Director. 20+ Years of Experience.

Note: The word (Working) has been added after the title because in very large global corporations, the Vice President and Director positions are strictly management roles that manage upwards and not downwards. These Directors are considered "Executive" Vice Presidents and Procurement Directors because they are not involved in the day to day management of categories or commodities. In a Small Business, the Vice President or Procurement Director would be considered "working" because of their involvement in day to day activities of the Procurement department.

Senior Category Manager – Responsible for the overall leadership and management of categories and commodities as well as procurement personnel. The Sr. Category Manager builds interdepartmental relationships; supervises personnel; prepares presentations for the Procurement Director; develops reports, policies and procedures; trains personnel; and is responsible for the performance of personnel, categories and commodities. Categories and commodities managed are strategic, high risk and/or high dollar. 15+ Years of Experience.

Category Manager – Responsible for the overall leadership and management of categories and commodities. The Category Manager is responsible for the performance of categories and commodities only and does not manage personnel. Medium risk and medium complex categories and commodities are managed by the Category Manager. 10+ Years of Experience.

Commodity Manager – Responsible for the overall management of one or more commodities. The Commodity Manager is responsible for the performance of the commodities. Only low to medium risk commodities are managed by the Commodity Manager; however, it is not unusual for a Commodity Manager to be a Subject Matter Expert (SME) in the commodity. Some SME examples are: energy, fuel, logistics, trucking, IT, raw materials, plastics, etc. SME Commodity Managers are typically in the Direct or COGs group because of the criticality of supply. 5+ Years of Experience.

Procurement Specialist – The Procurement Specialist is responsible for the performance of low risk/low dollar commodities. Examples are: office supplies, parking, janitorial, fencing, coffee, landscaping, etc. 2+ Years of Experience.

Contracts Administrator – The Contracts Administrator is responsible for the management of the Contract Management System (CMS). 1+ Years of Experience.

Buyer – Processes purchase orders on behalf of the BU. Responsible for minor negotiations on purchase orders up to a certain dollar threshold. Typically managed by the Director or a Sr. Category Manager. 1+ Years of Experience.

Expeditor – Responsible for the delivery and receipt of goods and/or services placed through a Purchase Order. 1+ Years of Experience.

Below is an example of an Organizational Chart for Procurement:

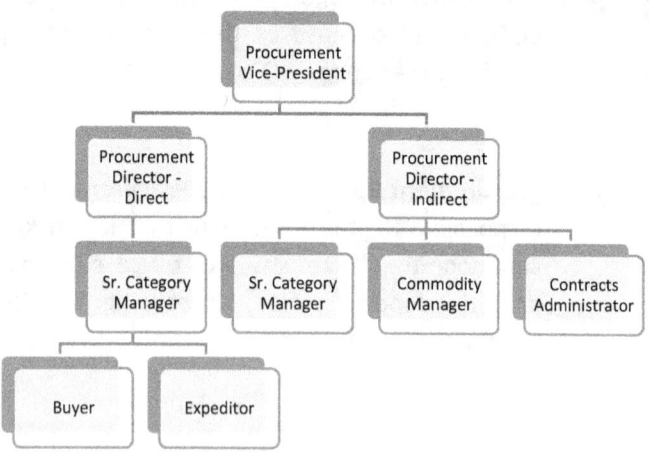

HOW TO HIRE THE RIGHT PEOPLE

Vice President or Procurement Director (Working) – Make sure the Vice-President or Director is a "working" Vice President or Director who has actively managed categories and commodities in their past few positions. Look for someone who has great people and project management skills as well as the experience and training to lead and manage the department.

Sr. Category Manager – The Sr. Category Manager's resume should be overflowing with training and experience managing a wide variety of personnel, categories and commodities. The Sr. Category Manager has to have at least some knowledge of almost every category in order to train and develop the personnel they supervise.

Commodity Manager – Unless the need is for an SME, the Commodity Manager should have managed at a least five to ten commodities in the past. The commodities should be diverse and be a mix of Direct and Indirect.

Procurement Specialist – The Procurement Specialist should have experience managing one to five or more commodities. The commodities should be diverse and be a mix of Direct and Indirect. Preferably, the

Procurement Specialist was promoted from Buyer or Contracts Administrator to Procurement Specialist.

Contracts Administrator – Monitors and records the flow of documents. Manages the Contract Management System (CMS) and makes sure all of the paperwork is completed for the contracts. Advises Category and Commodity Managers when contracts are expiring. May also prepare simple Amendments and Addendums.

Buyer – The Buyer should be comfortable negotiating pricing, managing the day-to-day activities of the purchase order system, and coordinating delivery with the Expeditor. Buyers are on the front line of controlling costs. Communication skills are essential for this position as the Buyer manages the day-to-day relationship with the vendors. Buyers are known for pulling rabbits out of hats.

Let's talk a minute about...

PULLING A RABBIT OUT OF A HAT

Pulling a rabbit out of hat is when a person does the unexpected and resolves a situation to the benefit of all. Some examples: Convincing a vendor to deliver outside of the promised delivery date; Negotiating down late fees for unpaid invoices; Convincing the vendor to change their production schedule without added costs, etc. Buyers are particularly good at this and are totally underappreciated when it happens. Go Buyers!

Expeditors – Expeditors are the right arms of the Buyers. They make numerous phone calls, send an avalanche of emails and deal with all sorts of upsets from overturned trucks to weather shutdowns. Look for a detail minded person with lots of common sense.

The best person to hire for a Small Business is the person who has worked in many of these positions. A Start Up or Small Business means that everyone wears multiple hats and pitches in to help as needed. A Small Business has no room for dead weight, slackers and people with egos. Everybody works hard and everybody contributes to the success of the company.

In Part I, Procurement was defined, the department structured, and personnel identified and hired. In Part II, we will discuss Procurement Policies and how Procurement interacts with the different departments within the Small Business.

PART II

PROCUREMENT POLICIES AND PROCESSES

PROCUREMENT POLICIES

A strong Procurement policy is essential to the success of the Procurement department and the Small Business. Too many companies say they don't want Procurement to constrain business; however, the lack of a clear Procurement policy results in confusion and allows the "Mavericks" to run wild. If Procurement does not have the support of the President and <u>all</u> members of the Leadership Team, it is doomed to limp along showing mediocre results. Remember, Procurement has no budget beyond their departmental expenses so their entire mandate is to help other departments succeed by controlling costs and squeezing the most value out of every dollar spent.

Let's talk a minute about...

MAVERICKS

Mavericks are the upper management people found in every company that believe rules are for other people. They also tend to encourage or at least tolerate this behavior in their direct reports. In their narcissistic world, mavericks believe that getting results trumps following the policies set forth by Procurement and other departments. Mavericks usually do not spend more than a couple of years at a company because they quit before their "brilliant" deals go south or are fired once these deals are recognized for the Martian dog doo they are and start to stink. The Maverick's actions result in production problems, paying too much, loss of revenue or a lawsuit; however, the Mavericks usually leave the company on a high note because they are smart enough to recognize when things are about to fall apart. Everybody else has to follow the policies and procedures except for them. Mavericks flourish at a company because of weak leadership by the President. Don't let it happen in your company!

The first step is to build a Procurement policy adhering to our mantra of Clear, Concise and Uncomplicated. Remember to have the right number and type of personnel to support any policy being rolled out. If the business is a Start-Up, you and your team of one or two people are the entire company so divvy up the responsibilities and watch out for these people as you grow. Look for an equitable distribution of responsibilities for personnel during a period of rapid growth. It does the company no good when one person is overburdened. Think temporary personnel and not permanent to get your company past these fast growth spurts and into a more stable and sustainable business environment.

Let's check in with the Martian Menagerie Company which has developed a simple Procurement policy.

MARTIAN MENAGERIE PROCUREMENT POLICY

1. <10,000GC (GC=Galactic Credits)

Annual combined spend for a vendor <10,000GC must be on the Martian Menagerie Short Form Contract template. No changes to the Short Form Contract are allowed. No exceptions! The vendor is responsible for filling out the contract in the highlighted sections and signing the contract. The tax ID form must be obtained by the BU and submitted with the vendor signed contract and proposal to the assigned Buyer for review and signature. If the vendor refuses to sign the short form contract, either find another vendor or contact the appropriate Category or Commodity Manager.

2. 10,000GC – 50,000GC

Annual combined spend for a vendor 10,000GC to 50,000GC proposal must be reviewed by the appropriate Procurement Category or Commodity Manager. Procurement will decide whether a Short Form or Full contract is used.

3. >50,000GC

Annual combined spend for a vendor that is >50,000GC requires making an appointment with the assigned Sr. Category Manager.

4. UNDER NO CIRCUMSTANCES SHOULD YOU...

- *Sign a quotation*
- *Sign a proposal*
- *Sign a contract*
- *Sign anything...you don't have the authority to commit the company to the financial obligation*
- *Have the vendor deliver goods or start work without a contract or purchase order*

If in doubt, please contact the Procurement Department.

We're here to help!

There are exactly 217 words in the Procurement Policy. Does it cover everything? Pretty much. There are always exceptions to the rule; however, it is up to Procurement to determine those exceptions. The exception decisions are rarely made in a vacuum and usually involve input from the BU, Legal and sometimes Finance. All exceptions to a process must be documented and followed. Too many times people work outside the established process; however, this behavior continues because there are no consequences to this bad behavior. Stop it! You, as the Start Up or Small Business owner, are in charge to make sure your people follow the established process. Be a leader!

CONTRACTS

Next, we are going to discuss the contract templates mentioned in the Procurement Policy. The three criteria normally used to evaluate what type of contract template should be used are Quantity, Cost and Risk.

CONTRACT EXAMPLES:

>10,000GC

A "Short Form" contract is a contract template for low quantity/low cost/low risk goods or services and should be no more than two or three pages plus the vendor proposal. Usually, the vendors signing these contracts are small businesses so terms and conditions should be kept to a minimum. Clear, Concise and Uncomplicated is definitely the rule here for both the seller and the buyer. The critical thing to remember is to make sure the Short Form Contract language contains language stating that the Short Form Contract prevails over any conflicting language in the vendor proposal, quotation and invoice.

>50,000GC

A complex or "Full" contract should be developed for high quantity/high-cost/high-risk contracts. These contracts always have the legal terms and conditions in the body of the contract and exhibits are added for Product, Services, Insurance, etc.

Note that there is nothing mentioned for the 10,000GC-50,000GC range. This is because Procurement should be consulted to determine which type of contract should be used.

CONTRACT EXAMPLES:

Office Supplies – High quantity/low-cost/low-risk contract – Full contract if delivering to 50+ locations, Short Form contract if local or less than 50 locations.

Statement of Work (SOW) to an existing contract to change out the gas meter – Low quantity/low-cost/high-risk – Full Contract because of the high risk involved in working on a gas line. Make sure the vendor has the appropriate vendor license, certification, and insurance certificate covering the work to be performed.

Coffee Supplies – Low quantity/low-cost/low-risk – Short Form Contract with attached pricing and schedule

Janitorial Services – low quantity/low-cost/high-risk – Full Contract because there should be background checks, confidentiality and other contractual language to reduce the risk of having unsupervised workers on site.

It is the responsibility of Procurement to negotiate the commercial and financial terms of a contract in conjunction with Supply Chain and Finance. Procurement translates the needs of the business into the commercial terms of the contract so that the contract reflects the intent and purpose set forth by the BU. If the contract terms and conditions cannot be understood by every party, as well as someone new to the negotiation, then the contract must be reworded until the intent and purpose is clear.

A contract can be reduced to the same three components that drive Procurement: Supply Chain, Finance and Legal. The breakdown of the contract is explained here:

1) **Supply Chain:** Pricing, Delivery and/or Statement of Work (Commercial Terms)

2) **Finance:** Payments, Returns (Credits), Payment Discounts, Payment Methods, etc. (Commercial Terms)

3) **Legal:** Indemnification, Liability, and a slew of other contractual language that mitigate risk (Legal Terms)

Let's talk a minute about...

CONTRACT RESPONSIBILITIES

Supply Chain and Finance are the owners of the Commercial Terms of a contract. Legal should not be involved in the Commercial Terms except to document the risk. Beware the lawyer who hi-jacks the contract and starts negotiating the Commercial Terms. Put a stop to this as quickly as possible as legal advice is always welcome but the risks should be identified and then accepted in writing by the BU or the Small Business Owner.

This is a great rule; however, there are always exceptions as set forth in this example: In order to cut costs, the BU agrees with the vendor that food containers will not be fitted with an anti-tamper proof sealant. This is an unacceptable risk and should not be accepted by the BU. In this case, legal counsel would overrule the BU decision to accept the risk. Common sense must prevail when evaluating risk.

If legal counsel is not on staff, a contracts lawyer should be hired to draft the Small Business contract templates. Do not, under any circumstances, hire the family lawyer who drafts the wills and trusts for a family owned business unless they are an expert in contracts. Different lawyers have different skills sets and the best is needed to draft the contract templates. The Small

Business owner depends on the language in these contract templates to protect the company. The contract templates are drafted once and then updated as needed; however, it is a good practice to have the contracts lawyer review the updated templates when major changes are made to the template or, at a minimum, annually. Most negotiations involve the commercial terms; however, some contracts can become very, very complicated.

If the Start-Up or Small Business owner is on a very limited budget, a variety of contract templates can be found on the internet at one of the many legal web sites. Shop around and choose the contract template that can be easily understood and is suitable for the state(s) in which the Small Business conducts business.

It is always preferable to use the Small Business contract template as it has been drafted to protect your Small Business and is, therefore, biased in favor of your company. The opposite is true if a vendor insists on using their contract template instead of the Small Business contract template. The assumption is that the contract is biased in favor of the vendor and it is Procurement's responsibility to mitigate the inherent risk of using another company's contract template.

When reviewing a contract, either the Small Business or vendor contract, redlines are applied to the document. A redline is the term used to track changes in a contract; however, the term is misleading because redlines can be any color depending on the settings in the computer program. Procurement should review the contract in conjunction with Supply Chain and make the first redlines to the commercial terms. After the first redlines are completed, the redlined contract is sent to legal counsel for their review and redline. It is Procurement's responsibility to coordinate all changes to the contract between Supply Chain, Finance, Legal, the vendor and the vendor's legal counsel. Conference calls between lawyers should be set up by Procurement and Procurement should always participate in the calls with Supply Chain and Finance as optional participants.

When building the Full Contract templates, it is best to build flexibility into the contract formation process. The best way of doing this is to create a Master Agreement with all the legal terms and conditions in the body of the contract and most commercial terms in the Exhibits. The exception to this rule is the Effective Date and Termination Date or Contract Term which are typically in the first section of the body of the contract. Effective Date is the date the contract becomes effective. Take care not to state the Effective Date as the date the contract was signed because people forget to date the contract. Effective Date pertains to the Master Contract; however, the accompanying Exhibits and Statements of Work may have different Effective Dates and Termination Dates specific to only those documents. Contract Term is the length of the contract and the language associated with notice of termination and contract default.

CONTRACT STRUCTURE

Let's look at the structure of several Full Contracts that the Martian Menagerie signed with several of their vendors:

EXAMPLE 1:

Martian Menagerie Products Agreement

Master Products Agreement

Exhibit A: Insurance Requirements

Exhibit B: Payment Terms & Procedures

Exhibit C: Product Pricing

Exhibit D: Stocking Agreement

Exhibit E: Delivery Pricing and Schedule

EXAMPLE 2:

Martian Menagerie Services Agreement

Master Services Agreement

Exhibit A: Insurance Requirements

Exhibit B: Payment Terms & Procedures

Exhibit C: Statement of Work

EXAMPLE 3:

Martian Menagerie Products & Services Agreement

Master Products & Services Agreement

Exhibit A: Insurance Requirements

Exhibit B: Statement of Work

Exhibit C: Product Parts Pricing

Exhibit D: Shipping & Delivery

EXAMPLE 4:

Martian Menagerie Services Agreement

Master Services Agreement

Exhibit A: Insurance Requirements

Exhibit B: Statement of Work

Notice the consistency between all four examples. The Master Agreement and Insurance Requirements are the first documents and will be common to all Full Contracts. The Master Agreement should contain only the legal terms and conditions as well as the Effective Date and Contract Termination language. Only the Exhibits will change with each contract depending on the products purchased and the services performed.

Amendments are used to change a contract and Addendums are used to add language to a contract. It is very easy to modify or add an Exhibit rather than to modify or change a Master Agreement. Once the Master Agreement has been approved by legal counsel, the Exhibits fall strictly within the responsibility of Procurement, Supply Chain and Finance. It is not necessary for legal counsel to review changes or additions to the Exhibits unless the Exhibits are modifying the Master Agreement terms and conditions. However, it is common for Statements of Work (SOWs) to override some of the terms and conditions of the Master Agreement. These SOWs should be reviewed by legal counsel if necessary.

Let's talk a minute about...

CONTRACTS

Once a contract is signed, it is rarely looked at unless there is a problem. If there is a problem, then the contract becomes the most important document in the world. Lawsuits are filed based on contract language and many millions of dollars have been lost or gained based on a vague clause or the placement of a comma. Treat a contract like the important document it is because it can be the life or death of the Small Business. Make sure the Commercial Terms in the contract are Clear, Concise and Uncomplicated. Both parties are obligated to perform to the terms of the contract; therefore, make sure the Small Business can meet the obligations of the contract. If the terms of the contract need to be adjusted, an addendum or amendment should be signed by both parties. Under no circumstances should changes be made to a document with a pen or pencil or agreed to in an email. Use an amendment or addendum to make the change.

SIGNING THE CONTRACT

Only people authorized by the owner or the board of directors should be authorized to sign a contract, commonly known as a Certificate of Incumbency or Financial Authority (FA). Certain people in the company are approved to commit the company to different levels of financial spend. For example, a Director may be able to sign contracts up to $100,000 or a Senior Vice President can sign up to $1,000,000. If the Small Business is a public company, a Certificate of Incumbency should be issued by the Board of Directors which lists the people authorized to legally bind the company by signing a contract. In addition, contracts should be signed digitally if possible. Signing digitally creates an online record of the contract, the person who signed the contract and the date it was signed. There are many companies that offer this online service; however, choose a vendor with a long history of signing and managing documents electronically.

CONTRACT MANAGEMENT

Now that the contract templates have been developed and vendors have signed the contracts, it is necessary to keep track of these important documents. A contract workflow process and accompanying procedure should be developed. There is nothing worse than being unable to find a contract or finding a contract has expired along with the negotiated pricing. An expired contract places the Small Business in a weak negotiation position and usually results in higher prices. It is better to start negotiations well before the contract expiration date so that there is time to take the products or services out to bid if necessary. Also, there may be automatic contract renewals written into the contract that need to be reviewed. For example, it is a disaster when a contract automatically renews for two years when the Strategic Sourcing Plan was to take the commodity out to bid or switch to another vendor.

Keeping with the mandate of Clear, Concise and Uncomplicated, the contract management process does not have to be complicated. There are several companies that offer Contract Management Systems (CMS) but these systems are very expensive. It is very easy to build a spreadsheet that tracks all of the necessary contract information. Some companies number their contracts; however, this is an option and not a requirement. Contracts are best tracked by the vendor name under one Master Contract. Amendments and Addendums are tracked subject to the Master Agreement.

Another option for building a CMS is to structure the CMS by category such as ENERGY, CONSTRUCTION, HUMAN RESOURCES, etc. Even if a vendor performs across multiple categories, there is most likely a separate contract or exhibit for each category. There is no set rule for a CMS except a contract should be able to be found upon the first search. Set up a system that works best for the Small Business but keep it consistent and keep it up to date.

Let's look at the Contract Management System (CMS) developed by the Martian Menagerie Company:

MARTIAN MENAGERIE CMS

The Martian Menagerie Company has a centralized web-based shared directory containing all signed contracts, Statements Of Work (SOW), vendor questionnaires, insurance certificates, etc. Contract folders are alphabetized by company name and access is restricted to Procurement and Legal Counsel. The Contract Management System (CMS) is an Excel spreadsheet and is managed by the Contracts Administrator in Procurement.

CMS SPREADSHEET COLUMNS:

Vendor Name

Contract Name (One line each for Master Agreement, Amendment 1, Addendum 1, Non-Disclosure Agreement, etc.)

Contract Type (Products, Services, Construction, Energy, Software, etc.)

Category

Effective Date

End Date

Termination Notice Date

Termination Notice Warning Date

Auto-Renew

Insurance Certificate Required (Yes/No)

Vendor Contact Name

Vendor Contact Phone Number

Vendor Contact Email

On the following page is an example of a simple CMS used by the Martian Menagerie Company.

	CONTRACTS			DATES						VENDOR INFORMATION		
VENDOR NAME	CONTRACT	TYPE	CATEGORY	EFFECTIVE	END	TERM NOTICE	AUTO RENEW	TERM WARNING	INSURANCE	NAME	PHONE	EMAIL
Martian Chugga Chugga Bowls	Master	Products	Direct	1/1/2030	12/31/2033	30 days	Yes	9/1/2033	Yes	Mike Jones	089-2877-34826	Mike@mccb.mars.com
Martian Chugga Chugga Bowls	Amend 1	Services	Indirect	1/4/2031	6/30/2031	N/A	No	N/A	No	Mike Jones	089-2877-34826	Mike@mccb.mars.com
Saturn Ring Bowls	Master	Products	Direct	3/1/2025	2/28/2028	60 days	Yes	11/1/2027	Yes	Marcie Smith	090-5298-22113	ms@satringbowls.satu.com

The spreadsheet columns in the CMS can be expanded or contracted as needed depending on the needs of the business. For example, if tracking insurance certificates is necessary for the Small Business, columns for the various insurance expiration dates should be added to the insurance section. It is best to have one person, such as a Contracts Administrator, manage the flow of documents and notices. In a small company, this should be the responsibility of the most junior person in Procurement because it is such a good training tool to learn about the different vendors and contracts.

At the start of any relationship with a vendor, a Non-Disclosure Agreement and a Vendor Questionnaire should be filled out and kept with the contract file. A thorough Vendor Questionnaire can tell the Small Business Owner everything he or she needs to know about a vendor.

VENDOR QUESTIONNAIRE

The Vendor Questionnaire is a simple spreadsheet with the following questions:

Company Name:

Company Address:

Contact Name:

Contact Phone:

Contact Email:

Public or Private:

Is the company a subsidiary of another company?

Does the company own or have part ownership in other companies?

Number of Employees:

Where does the company rank against similar companies in the same industry?

Top 3 Competitors (Sales):

Membership in Trade Associations:

Has the company won any Industry Awards?

If yes, please explain:

Annual Sales $:

Top 3 Customers in order by $:

Top 3 Customers in order by % of Total Sales:

Has the company under this name or a previous name ever filed bankruptcy?

Main Products and/or Services Offered:

Are Sub-Contractors used to perform the Services?

If yes, how are Sub-Contractors used?

Is the company currently in litigation?

If yes, please explain:

VENDOR QUESTIONNAIRE

DATE:	
COMPANY NAME:	
COMPANY ADDRESS:	
CONTACT NAME:	
CONTACT PHONE:	
CONTACT EMAIL:	
Public or Private?	
Is the company a subsidiary of another company?	
Does the company own or have part ownership in other companies?	
Number of Employees:	
Where does the company rank against similar companies in the same industry?	
Top 3 Competitiors:	
Membership in Trade Associations:	
Has the company won any Industry Awards?	
If yes, please explain:	
Annual Sales:	
Top 3 Customers by $:	
Top 3 Customers in order by % of Sales:	
Has the company under this name or a previous name ever filed bankruptcy?	
Main Products and/or Services Offered:	
Are Sub-Contractors used to perform the Services?	
If yes, how are Sub-Contractors used?	
Is the company currently in litigation?	
If yes, please explain:	

Questions can be added to customize the Vendor Questionnaire suitable for the Small Business. Some examples of customization are Return Rates on Products, Customer Retention Rates, On Time Delivery Metrics, etc. Since the Vendor Questionnaire will be stored electronically with the contract, the information is particularly useful when there has been a change in personnel within Procurement or a new Category or Commodity Manager has taken over the vendor relationship.

Below are some more details on why these questions are asked on the Vendor Questionnaire:

VENDOR QUESTIONNAIRE

Company Name:

BASIC INFORMATION

Company Address:

BASIC INFORMATION

Contact Name:

BASIC INFORMATION

Contact Phone:

BASIC INFORMATION

Contact Email:

BASIC INFORMATION

Website Address:

BASIC INFORMATION

Public or Private:

NEGOTIATIONS & FINANCIALS: Usually, a private company will not disclose sales figures. The owner will be the President or CEO which means this person is the Decision Maker. Identifying the Decision Maker is a critical component of a successful negotiation. A public company will list their financials, stock price, etc. on their website.

Is the company a subsidiary of another company?

BASIC INFORMATION & NEGOTIATIONS: This vendor may already be doing business with your company under a different subsidiary name but it was unknown until now. Leverage can be gained to lower prices by becoming a larger customer in the eyes of the vendor if spend can be combined from two different subsidiaries of the same parent company.

Does the company own or have part ownership in other companies?

SEE PREVIOUS ANSWER.

Number of Employees:

BASIC INFORMATION: Gives a good estimate of the size and depth of the company. A broker may have a small number of employees but a database of thousands of "sub-contractors" or "affiliates" or "partners".

Where does the company rank against similar companies in the same industry?

RISK & NEGOTIATIONS: Vendors are very sensitive (or proud) of their performance against their direct competitors. If the answer is Number 2 then the company is eager to become Number 1 especially if they were Number 1 previously. This information may be a negotiation fulcrum to gain better pricing, service, etc. When the vendor answers this question, it is up to Procurement to determine if the question is answered at a local, state, regional or national level. For example, if the Small Business is sourcing landscaping in Atlanta and there are seven vendor facilities in the Atlanta, Georgia area, then the strength of a local or metro presence in Atlanta is more desirable rather a larger number of facilities located nationwide but not concentrated in the Atlanta area.

Membership in Trade Associations:

PERFORMANCE: This is actually a very good indicator of the professionalism of the company. Bonus points for employees who serve on boards of the trade organizations or sit on committees that set the standards for their industry. This means the vendor has made a long term commitment to the industry and has sought out the experts...and hired them.

Has the company won any Industry Awards?

PERFORMANCE: Has the vendor won awards for Customer Service, On-Time Delivery, etc. These are good indicators of performance. Just like a good bottle of wine...look for the medals on the label.

If yes, please explain:

SEE PREVIOUS ANSWER

Top 3 Competitors:

NEGOTIATIONS & SOURCING: Use this information to find out the other vendors you should be speaking with if this vendor is not suitable. Also, it is a good indication of the vendors who should be invited to the next Request for Proposal (RFP) for this commodity.

Annual Sales $:

FINANCIAL: Speaks to the size of the company.

Top 3 Customers in order by $:

RISK & FINANCIAL: Speaks to the size of the company. Look for well-known large corporations amongst their customers. If large corporations are listed amongst a vendor's customers, then the vendor is able to meet strict criteria in performance, price, and delivery. Most large corporations are a pain to deal with and are not considered easy money. Vendors work with large corporations at ridiculously low margins because of two reasons: 1) Profit (high volume/low margin), and 2) the marketing value when selling to other higher paying smaller customers. If the vendor can work with these large corporations and succeed, then the infrastructure and processes are already in place to handle the Small Business and its rapid growth.

Top 3 Customers in order by % of Total Sales:

RISK & FINANCIAL: This is probably one of the most crucial questions that the vendor must answer. If 80% of their sales is with one customer and that customer decides to move to another vendor or goes out of business, then the risk is extremely high that the vendor will go out of business. Look for a good mix such as 10%, 8% and 12% for the top three customers. No customer should be more that 25% of the business with the vendor.

Has the company, under this name or a previous name, ever filed bankruptcy?

RISK & FINANCIAL: If the answer is yes, it is a red flag but not necessarily a deal killer. Many large corporations emerge like phoenixes from bankruptcy as they shed debt or sell off unprofitable divisions or subsidiaries.

Main Products and/or Services Offered:

BASIC INFORMATION: This is a good question that often surprises since the vendor has previously only talked about X, Y and Z products but didn't know the Small Business was also looking for products A, B and C. Consolidation of spend with successfully performing vendors is good for the Small Business because consolidation turns the Small Business into a larger account which, in turn, creates greater leverage in negotiations.

Are Sub-Contractors used to perform the Services?

RISK: If the answer is yes, then a Full Contract is required. Sometimes, Supply Chain is so focused on the development of the SOW that they forget to ask this very important question. Risk is extremely high when sub-contractors are used.

If yes, how are Sub-Contractors used?

RISK: If Sub-Contractors are only used on a case by case basis such as when a crane or special equipment is rented, then the risk is lower but still requires a Full Contract. If a General Contractor (GC) is hired for a Construction Contract, then the answer to the question about sub-contractors would be 90% or 95% since electricians, plumbers, etc. are not employees of the GC. This is standard for the construction industry; however, the flow-down language in the contract needs to be very precise and robust.

Is the company currently in litigation?

RISK: If the case is lost, will it throw the company into bankruptcy? Proceed with caution.

If yes, please explain:

SEE PREVIOUS ANSWER

This concludes Part II. In Part III, Strategic Sourcing will be defined and Martian Menagerie will conduct a Request For Proposal (RFP).

PART III

STRATEGIC SOURCING
&
REQUEST FOR PROPOSAL

STRATEGIC SOURCING

Strategic Sourcing is a phrase that has caught on in the past few years but few people truly understand what it means. Keeping with our mantra of Clear, Concise and Uncomplicated, the following meaning best describes "Strategic Sourcing":

"The planned acquisition of goods or services from specific vendors as part of a long term vendor management strategy to reduce costs, mitigate risk and improve performance."

Procurement personnel have always performed strategic sourcing and most people do it subconsciously on a personal level. A person shopping for new living room furniture will look at the different models and options and then shop around for the best price. This person checks out the stores, warranty, delivery or pickup, or will perhaps shop online. If this person is a negotiator, he or she may be able to convince the store owner to throw in some coffee tables, free delivery, extended warranty or 0% financing as part of the deal. This is Strategic Sourcing.

Strategic Sourcing is inherently tied to a Request For Proposal (RFP) or a Request For Quotation (RFQ). A RFQ is just a shorter version of a RFP focusing on specific products or services only. Since the RFP is more comprehensive we are going to focus on the process of conducting an RFP.

REQUEST FOR PROPOSAL

The most common number of steps in a Request For Proposal (RFP) is seven; however, this is not a set rule. A RFP can be a long, drawn out affair with a significant commitment made by multiple departments of time and manpower, therefore, major RFPs should only be conducted for a significant amount of spend. Let's go visit the Martian Menagerie Company and check out their strategic sourcing plan for buying the food bowls for the various animals shipped throughout the galaxy.

MARTIAN MENGAGERIE

FOOD BOWLS REQUEST FOR PROPOSAL

RFP SUMMARY

The current situation for food bowls involves eight vendors in geographically diverse places throughout the galaxy. Currently, the food bowls do not always meet specifications which generates returns to the manufacturer; however, production will ship a sub-par quality food bowl rather than go through the rather onerous returned goods process. Bowl deliveries from the current vendors are often early which causes problems because of the lack of warehouse space to store early deliveries. Late deliveries also cause production delays which, in turn, may cause late deliveries to the customer. In addition, exorbitant expedited shipping fees are often incurred as the result of late deliveries to the customer. Spend is approximately 810,000GC (GC=Galactic Credits) per year.

The Strategic Sourcing plan is to reduce the current vendors from eight to two or possibly three. The goals are to:

1) Leverage consolidated spend to reduce costs for product and delivery
2) Reduce on-time delivery failures
3) Streamline returns of defective products
4) Improve the warranty from 30 days to 60 days
5) Upgrade the specifications of the food bowls

6) Introduce penalties for early/late deliveries and defective products
7) Savings goal of >8% of current costs

RFP STEPS ONE THROUGH SEVEN

STEP ONE

IDENTIFY THE RFP TEAM MEMBERS

Identify the RFP team members and assign roles

Develop the timeline for the RFP

STEP TWO

DEFINE THE SCOPE OF THE RFP

Define the scope of the RFP

STEP THREE

IDENTIFY RFP VENDORS

List the current vendors and identify new vendors

STEP FOUR

PREPARE THE RFP VENDOR PACKET

Prepare the RFP packet for vendors

STEP FIVE

REVIEW & SCORE VENDOR PROPOSALS

RFP team reviews the vendor proposals

Vendor scorecard matrix is developed

Vendor list is narrowed to finalists

Site visits are made to vendors' manufacturing facilities

STEP SIX

VENDOR PRESENTATIONS & AWARDS

Vendor Presentations

Scoring of vendors

Awards of business

STEP SEVEN

TRANSITION TO NEW VENDORS

Contract signed

Transition from old vendors to new vendors (if necessary)

RFP STEP ONE

Identify the RFP team members and assign roles.

Members of the RFP team will include the following people:

Procurement:

>Sr. Category Manager (RFP Team Leader)
>
>Buyer (Document Control)

Supply Chain:

>Production
>
>Technical Owner/Quality Control (QA)
>
>Receiving/Shipping (Delivery)

Finance:

>Supervisor or team leader in either Accounts Payable or Accounts Receivable (Finance)

Legal:

>Legal Counsel (optional)

A senior member of the Procurement department such as the Director or Senior Category Manager should always lead a major RFP. Category and Commodity managers or Procurement Specialists and Buyers should be added to major RFP teams because these are excellent training opportunities to develop skills in negotiations and to get a first-hand look at how to lead an inter-departmental team.

Let's talk a minute about...

LEADING INTER-DEPARTMENTAL TEAMS

Inter-departmental teams are the most difficult of all teams to lead as each member has their own agenda and priorities. It is Procurement's job to balance all of these needs, which are sometimes conflicting, and translate them into a successful RFP. Team members negotiate with each other as the RFP progresses with give-and-take between the different departments; however, the RFP Team Leader has the final say on the results of the internal negotiations.

One example of an internal negotiation between RFP team members is a discussion between Supply Chain and Finance on vendor payment terms. If all RFP vendors require 30-day payment terms, the compromise between the standard Small Business 60-day payment term and the vendor's 30 day payment term may be a 2% discount offered on 30 days payment. Another compromise would be to split the difference and offer the vendor 45 day payment terms.

Set the timeline for the RFP

An RFP should not last more than three months from start to finish. The RFP can be shorter but it is a rush for everyone in a major RFP, particularly vendors, to finish in less than three months. Month 1 can be shortened if this is a repeat RFP and RFP document templates are used, all historical data has been collected, and data analysis has been done before the RFP starts. The trick is to get everyone to the table as business travel and vacation schedules intervene. If an RFP team member is on vacation or traveling on business, their duties should be delegated to one of their senior people so that this person does not break the forward momentum of the RFP.

FOOD BOWL RFP TIMELINE

MONTH 1

Identification of team members, assignment of roles and communication of schedule to everyone

Historical data is listed on a detailed product spend spreadsheet covering the past 12 months

Identification of RFP vendor participants

Preparation of Vendor RFP Packet

Review and approval of Vendor RFP Packet by team members

MONTH 2

Vendor RFP Packet sent to all vendors with deadline for response within three weeks

Team review of vendor proposals

Narrowing of vendor list to finalists

Vendor site visits to finalists (if necessary)

MONTH 3

Presentations by vendors

Awards of business

Contracts signed

Implementation

RFP STEP TWO

Define the scope of the RFP

Products are limited to Food Bowls only

Large Bowls, 6 styles, metal, 150,000GC

Medium Bowls, 12 styles, metal and plastic, 512,000GC

Small Bowls, 4 styles, ceramics, 148,000GC

Total: 22 styles, 810,000GC

Let's talk a minute about...

SCOPE CREEP

Scope creep is when the original RFP for food bowls suddenly expands to include bedding, locks and the kitchen sink. Unless there is a legitimate and financial reason why additional products or services are added to the RFP, the RFP Procurement Team leader should shut down all scope creep. A good example of an allowed Scope Creep is the addition of Food Bowl Utensils because some manufacturers ship the Food Bowl and Utensil as a bundled item.

RFP STEP THREE

List the current vendors and identify new vendors.

CURRENT VENDORS

Martian Chugga Chugga Bowls

Saturn Ring Bowls

Martian Specialty Plastics

Venus VaVaVoom Bowls

Lunar Dishes

Martian Monster Metals

Mercury Military Equipment

Mega Martian Metals

NEW VENDORS:

Martian Materials Distribution

Mellie's Martian Food Bowls

Incumbent vendors should always be invited to the RFP even if the intent is to remove them as vendors. During the course of an RFP, an incumbent vendor may be surprised to learn that their company's performance is not meeting their customer's expectations. This disconnect between reality and the vendor's perception of reality is quite distinct and is a wake-up call that the vendor is in danger of losing the business. The RFP presentation is an opportunity for the incumbent vendor to correct their mistakes and lay out a Corrective Action Plan (CAP) in their RFP response.

RFP STEP FOUR

Prepare the RFP packet for vendors

The RFP packet is electronic and can be conducted by email since this is the simplest way. Many professional purchasing groups offer websites to conduct an RFP with log-ins and passwords for the vendors; however, there is a cost associated with this which is usually prohibitive for a Small Business.

FOOD BOWL RFP PACKET FOR PARTICIPANTS

Summary of purpose in conducting the RFP

Vendor rules for the RFP

Timeline of the RFP

Deadline for questions

Historical data

Format for submitting pricing

Deadline for proposal submission

Finalists chosen

Vendor Presentations

Award of Business

Let's peruse the food bowls RFP packet prepared by the Martian Menagerie Company to send to their vendors.

VENDOR FOOD BOWL RFP PACKET

(Including Author's Notes)

SUMMARY OF PURPOSE

The current situation for food bowls involves eight vendors in geographically diverse places throughout the galaxy. The food bowls do not always meet specifications which generates returns to the manufacturer; however, production will ship a sub-par quality food bowl rather than go through the rather onerous return goods process. Bowl deliveries are often early which causes problems because of the lack of warehouse space to store early deliveries. Late deliveries also cause production delays which, in turn, cause late deliveries to the customer. Exorbitant expedited shipping fees to the customer are often the result of late deliveries.

Spend is approximately 810,000 GC (GC=Galactic Credits) per year. The RFP for the Food Bowls is <u>not</u> a "winner take all" situation and it is the Martian Menagerie Company's intention to consolidate into two vendors: primary and secondary. If necessary, sole source and specialty vendors may also be chosen to supplement the primary and secondary vendors.

VENDOR & BU RULES

Vendors are forbidden to discuss the RFP with any employee of the company except the Procurement RFP Team Leader. Incumbent vendors are instructed to discuss only the day to day business needs with the BU. Both vendors and company employees are instructed to direct all questions concerning the RFP to the Procurement RFP Team Leader. No new large orders for products are to be placed by the BU during the timeline for the RFP without the express written consent of the Procurement RFP Team Leader.

RFP TIMELINE

MONTH 1

Identification of team members, assignment of roles and communication of schedule

Historical data is listed on a detailed product spend spreadsheet for past 12 months

Identification of RFP vendor participants

Preparation of Vendor RFP Packet

Review and approval of Vendor RPF Packet by RFP team members

MONTH 2

Vendor RFP Packet sent to all vendors with deadline for response within three weeks

Team review of vendor proposals

Narrowing of vendor list to finalists

Vendor site visits to finalists (if necessary)

Awards of business

Implementation

QUESTIONS & ANSWERS (Q&A)

All questions must be submitted by (date) and all answers will be distributed to all vendors at the same time.

Q & A NOTES:

An important part of the RFP is the Question and Answer period. This is usually from one to three weeks long. If the RFP is well written, there will not be many questions; however, a poorly written RFP will generate numerous questions because the vendors do not have clear instructions or the historical data is flawed. All questions and responses are collated by the Procurement RFP Team Leader and distributed to ALL vendors at the same time so that no company has an unfair advantage. Frequency of the communication is at least once per week; however, it can be more or less frequent if necessary. It is crucial that a fair and unbiased platform for the questions and answers be maintained.

HISTORICAL DATA AND FORECAST

See spreadsheet attachment.

HISTORICAL DATA AND FORECAST NOTES

An in-depth analysis of food bowl and accessories spend is conducted by Procurement. The analysis should show, at a minimum, the following:

Total Spend for the past three years

Spend by vendor

Product list including Quantity, Price, Specification and Total Spend for each vendor

If necessary, other columns such as location, delivery costs, custom fees, delivery times, etc. can be added. This information becomes the template for the RFP response by the vendors. The pricing is blanked out and filled in by the vendors when submitting their bid proposal. Projected purchase quantities for the upcoming year(s) should also be provided to the vendor.

DEADLINE FOR RFP RESPONSE

Vendor responses are due by (date)

DEADLINE FOR RFP RESPONSE NOTES

There is no set timeline for vendor responses to an RFP; however, vendors prefer at least three weeks to a month to prepare their response. The timeline is as long or as short as it needs to be.

FINALIST NOTIFICATIONS

Vendor finalists will be notified by (date)

RFP FINALIST NOTIFICATIONS NOTES

The Procurement team leader calls each vendor and notifies them that they are cut or have made it to the vendor presentations.

VENDOR PRESENTATIONS

Vendors should keep their calendar free the week of (date). Dress code for the presentation is business dress. Each vendor is allotted 50 minutes for their presentation including set up. Please send your Audio/Visual (A/V) requirements to the RFP Procurement Team Leader.

VENDOR PRESENTATIONS NOTES

A tentative date is set for vendor presentations. Usually vendors are asked to hold that week open;

however, this date may be adjusted according to business and vendor needs. It is no use scheduling the vendor presentations when the annual galactic food bowl convention is going on at the same time.

AWARDS OF BUSINESS

Vendors will be notified of awards of business by (date).

AWARDS OF BUSINESS NOTES

The Award Date may be delayed due to recognized gaps of information in the vendor presentations. A second round of presentations by one or more vendors is sometimes required.

RFP STEP FIVE

Proposals reviewed by RFP team & Vendor Scorecard Matrix developed

The Procurement RFP Team Leader collates all the bids received in the proposals, creates the vendor scoring matrix, and writes up a brief analysis of each vendor's RFP response. The RFP team meets to discuss each vendor bid and weights the sections of the scoring matrix accordingly. For example, on time delivery may be more important than customer service or price may be more important than delivery time. A vendor scoring matrix takes the emotion out of the evaluation and forces everyone on the RFP team to quantify their opinions of the intangibles such as "ease of doing business" and "customer service".

Vendor list narrowed to finalists

The vendor scoring matrix is used to rank the vendors in descending order with the top three vendors invited to give presentations.

Site visits made to vendor manufacturing facilities

Once the finalists have been identified and notified, site visits to the vendor's manufacturing facilities may be necessary. A "Vendor Site Visit" form and scoring matrix should be created so that the same questions, observations and evaluations are given to all vendors.

RFP STEP SIX

Vendor Presentations

Vendors give their presentations based on the criteria set forth on the vendor scorecard. Each section of their presentation should match the scorecard with the last slide showing their "added value". "Added Value" is that special something that sets them apart from the competition. The audience should be made up of all members of the RFP team plus any decision makers such as the Vice President of Supply Chain and the President.

Scoring of vendors

Each member of the audience fills in their scorecard after each vendor presentation. The scores are collated and the decision is made. In a critical products or services RFP, primary vendor and secondary vendors should be chosen. The goal is to have 80% of the business go to the primary vendor and 20% go to the secondary vendor. Sole source or specialty vendors can also be "winners" although the percentage of spend is usually very small.

Let's talk a minute about...

PARETO and his magical 80/20 rule

I'm not going to bore everyone with the history of Pareto...let's just say he was an incredibly smart fellow back when horses were the preferred mode of transportation and Mars was known as the God of War rather than a planet. If further research on Pareto's 80/20 rules is necessary, the internet will tell you everything. Remember, the 80/20 rule is not an exact science, it could be 82/18 or 77/23 so don't get too hung up on the precise numbers. Procurement uses the 80/20 rule extensively when performing analysis of historical spend data but it is amazing how often this rule also applies to other situations. Another good example of Pareto's rule is 80% of sales is generated by 20% of the customers.

Awards of business to vendors

The Procurement RFP team leader calls each vendor and notifies them of the results of the presentations.

RFP STEP SEVEN

Contracts are signed

Every effort should be made to make sure the vendor's presentation promises are reflected in the contract language. For example, if the vendor's top selling point was free delivery on pallet orders, this language should be added to the Statement Of Work (SOW) in the contract. Do not start moving the business from the incumbent vendor to the new vendor until the contract is signed by both parties.

Transition from old vendors to new vendors

The transition from one vendor to another can be a very difficult time for both the company and the vendor. In complicated RFPs such as HealthCare or the outsourcing Payroll, both contracts for the incumbent and new vendor should contain transition clauses. This language protects the Small Business as it moves from one vendor to another and reduces the complications inherent in moving a complicated category or commodity to a new vendor. There is no set time period for transition; however, most complicated contract transition clauses stipulate at least 90 or 120 days for the transition period and downloading of historical data. For example, moving outsourced payroll from one company to another involves coordinating the Human Resources, Finance and Information Technology departments. So much is dependent on the "electronic hand-shaking" that goes on between a vendor and the business that test runs are necessary to make sure data is transmitted correctly and at the right time.

The successful transition from the old to the new vendor and the realized savings means the RFP was successful. One month after the RFP is completed, a wrap up RFP team meeting should be held to identify what worked and what didn't. Best Practices should be identified and communicated to all appropriate members of Procurement, Supply Chain, Finance and Legal. Three months after the transition is completed, a Quarterly Business Review (QBR) with the vendor should be held to make sure everyone is still on track in accomplishing the goals of the RFP first laid out in the RFP summary.

This concludes Part III. In Part IV, the discussion will focus on Reporting, Negotiations, and How to Work with a Large Corporation.

PART IV

REPORTING, NEGOTIATIONS & HOW TO WORK WITH A LARGE CORPORATION

REPORTING

Reporting is one of the most important tools used to control costs and grow the Small Business. If the Small Business does not know where the money is being spent each month, how can anyone know where to reduce costs, leverage consolidation of spend, and forecast for the future?

The finance department should be running a monthly report of all the money spent during the course of the month (Spend Report). The Spend Report should show the Vendor, Date, Amount Paid, Delivery Location, etc. This report should be available to multiple departments including Supply Chain and Procurement. The ideal way to do this is to give each department "view only" access to the system database. The fields or columns should be customizable depending on what information is necessary to that department.

Different departments view the same information but interpret the data differently but relevant to what they do. In the case of Procurement, it is vital to track spend with vendors and identify opportunities for future contracts. A vendor that signed a Short Form Contract for under 50,000GC but is now trending upwards to 100,000GC should be reviewed by Procurement to see if there is an opportunity to reduce costs. This upward trend with a vendor should trigger a conversation with Supply Chain to discuss whether this is a short term trend or a long term strategic shift from a primary vendor to a secondary vendor. It is not unheard of for a primary vendor to get into a parts shortage situation which necessitates shifting orders to the secondary vendor. If the situation is projected to continue, then either a stocking agreement should be added to the contract with the primary vendor or a negotiation should take place with the secondary vendor to forecast increased supply and leverage lower prices.

Another reason for Procurement to review the monthly spend is to make sure major vendors are being paid on time. It is a red flag when a contract has been signed, orders are flowing in but no payments are being made to the vendor. The last thing a company wants to do is get into an "aging" situation with a vendor. Invoices past due skews the financial reporting which makes the company's financial position look better than it really is. More than one executive has been blindsided by skewed financial reporting based on vendor billing issues.

If the Small Business is involved in manufacturing, Procurement relies heavily on the inventory and manufacturing reports. This is particularly true if Min/Max levels are set in the computer system for computerized ordering of parts from vendors. Stocking agreements are also based on these reports and if usage is faster or slower than projected for the stocking agreement, a re-negotiation with the vendor may be necessary. This is particularly important when there is a minimum usage or minimum purchase commitment in the contract.

Let's talk a minute about...

GARBAGE IN / GARBAGE OUT

Reports are the lifeblood of every company so remember the old computer programmer's adage: Garbage In / Garbage Out. It is no use relying on a report that is full of inaccuracies. A good Category or Commodity Manager can take one look at a report, either financial or manufacturing, and know whether it is in line with signed contracts and forecasted projections. One of the easiest things for a leader to do is let inaccurate information creep into the database. Business decisions are based on the information in reports; therefore, it should be everybody's responsibility to make sure the data is accurate.

Author's Note: In this chapter, because Negotiations are between individuals and not between companies, the second person "you" and "yours" has been used.

NEGOTIATIONS

There are many books and articles written about How to Negotiate; How to win, Win, WIN at every Negotiation; and You're a LOSER if you don't WIN! We should ALL BE WINNERS! That's just plain silly. There is no trophy at the finish line of negotiations otherwise it would be called a RACE!

In a negotiation, the WIN is predicated on your own definition of success

Someone else may think you lost the negotiation but in your mind you've achieved a successful result to the negotiation. Who is to say you are right or wrong? No one but you!

Let's talk a minute about...

NEGOTIATING WITH CONFIDENCE

Successful negotiations are all about confidence. You cannot let the other side know you are in a poor negotiating position. You should walk into a negotiation as if you have the world in your pocket. It's amazing how this attitude affects your entire demeanor from the moment you enter the room to the moment you leave. Good negotiators can smell weakness! And don't tell me you can't negotiate; everyone has grown up negotiating. Remember when your mother or father first said "NO" and you didn't take "NO" for an answer, you started whining and crying and stomping your little feet. THAT was your first negotiation for getting what you wanted. So be Confident when you walk into a negotiation because you've been doing this all of your life!

In keeping with our mandate of Clear, Concise and Uncomplicated, the negotiation process has been broken down into four simple steps. Then we're going to hop across the galaxy and follow the Martian Menagerie team as they negotiate the food bowl prices as part of the RFP.

NEGOTIATION STEPS

1. Knowledge
2. Pre-Negotiation Planning
3. Negotiation
4. The Deal

1. Knowledge

The one consistent theme throughout negotiation training is knowledge. The more you know, the more leverage (power) you have.

Knowledge can be broken down into the following:

What are the known facts about the adversary?

What are the facts that are known only by you?

What are the facts known by both sides?

What are your assumptions?

What are the adversary's assumptions?

How can I leverage the facts and assumptions to negotiate the best deal?

Let's talk a minute about...

ASSUMPTIONS

Assumptions are made when all of the facts are unknown. Facts are identified and then extrapolated to a future projection which is the assumption. If you get the basic facts wrong, the incorrect assumptions and decisions multiply exponentially. Too many bad deals are made and contracts signed based on incorrect assumptions. Turn the assumptions into facts!

Below are a couple of the most common assumptions made during a RFP:

Example 1:
Assumption: Shipping costs are included in the price quoted
Fact: Shipping costs are not included which raises the price quoted by 15%

Example 2:
Assumption: Warranty claims on the product are the responsibility of the distributor
Fact: Warranty claims are made against the manufacturer of the product and not against the distributor

---

2. Pre-Negotiation Planning

In order to plan your strategy for the negotiation, the following questions should be asked and answered for both your side and the adversary's side. Assign a RFP team member to answer on behalf of the adversary.

Pre-Negotiation Questions:

What are the goals of the negotiation?

At what point will this negotiation be considered successful?

What are the talking points?

What should NOT be discussed?

What is the fallback position?

What is the walk away position?

Who will lead the negotiation?

Who will be at the negotiation table?

What are their titles and roles?

Who will be the "Mystery Manager"?

What will be the tone and mood?

What are the trigger words for breaks and step backs?

What is the setting and seating arrangements?

What are the props?

Let's talk a minute about...

THE "MYSTERY MANAGER"

If you've ever bought a car or tried to arrange free delivery for some furniture or some similar personal product, invariably, the salesperson will say, "Let me check with my manager." This may be a real person or it may be a figment of the salesperson's imagination. Most of the time, you will not know because you rarely see the "Mystery Manager." Don't let it fake you out. Sometimes it is true and you're dealing with the lowest man on the totem pole who has absolutely no authority to grant your wish. Other times, the person you're speaking with is the "Mystery Manager" and he really wants to get a cup of coffee or take a bathroom break. No matter what...go with the flow and don't let them get under your skin. One of my favorite ploys is to ask to speak to the "Mystery Manager" directly. Usually, you are denied an audience with the "all powerful" Mystery Manager but it will give you some satisfaction to see the salesperson squirm and make up excuses on why you can't meet with the Mystery Manager. Occasionally, the Mystery Manager does appear and you can quickly come to an agreement without the salesperson playing middle man; however, this is rare because the "Mystery Manager" is almost always fictional and a negotiating ploy. Recognize it for what it is and adjust accordingly.

3. Negotiation

You've done your homework, everybody knows their roles, you've practiced, and you're here to get the job done. During the negotiation you must:

Establish control immediately so speak first and act the host. Ask everyone if they are comfortable, need anything to drink, etc. This establishes the fact that you are the host and, therefore, the person to please. Make the introductions of your team including titles and roles and then ask the lead negotiator to do the same for their side. Some vendors will speak first and take over the host role because they want to establish themselves as being in control. Don't be rude...go with the flow. Negotiations are all about constant adjustments so be prepared to be flexible and don't let it rattle you.

Go over the agenda and the goals of the meeting making sure everyone is clear on what is to be achieved at this meeting.

Ask for the name of the ultimate decision maker and if that person is at the meeting. If the decision maker is not at the meeting (this is common), do not get upset and adjust accordingly. Some companies, including the Small Business, require a C-Level executive, President or Owner to sign off on all deals.

During the introductory period, you are setting the tone and mood (antagonistic, conciliatory, enthusiastic, bored, etc.).

Allow the other team to speak first. This will put them at their ease since they want to get things out in the open as soon as possible. The person or team that speaks first usually says more than they should and this information can help you during the negotiation. Let them take all the time in the world. Take notes and don't ask too many questions. Watch the body language and take note if the speaker keeps looking to someone else on their team for validation. This is the person with the most power on their team.

When it is your turn to speak, stick to your talking points but be prepared to adjust your agenda if circumstances warrant. Since you've allowed the other party to speak first and present their case, you know more than them. Remember, knowledge is power.

After an agreement has been reached, do NOT commit to anything at this stage. You can "tentatively" commit if the numbers meet or exceed your negotiation goals but do not say, "We have a Deal!" That only happens on game shows.

If negotiations are not going well, reset the negotiation. Use bathroom breaks, urgent phone calls, validation of numbers, talk to your "Mystery Manager", etc. to break up the tension. Lunch is always a good idea and reconvening either in the afternoon or the next day can bring a fresh perspective and attitude to the negotiation.

4. The Deal

Once everybody has spoken and there is a tentative deal in place, the negotiation is concluded and the real work begins. Before the meeting ends, decide which party will summarize the points of the agreement and prepare the first draft of the contract. Make sure notes were taken during the negotiation so that these points can be checked against the contract draft.

Let's check in on the Martian Menagerie as they negotiate with the RFP food bowl winner.

MARTIAN MENAGERIE FOOD BOWL NEGOTIATION

All of the presentations were given by the top scoring vendors of the Food Bowl RFP and the decision, supported by the RFP Vendor Scorecard, was made to give the majority of the business to the Martian Materials Distribution Corporation.

Martian Materials Distribution Corporation is a large corporation publicly traded on the Martian Stock Exchange under the abbreviation MEGM. Annual sales top 225 billion GC (Galactic Credits) and MEGM employs over 250,000 people throughout the galaxy.

The focus and effort should be on steps 1 and 2 as these are the most important steps in a successful negotiation.

1. Knowledge

What are the known facts about MEGM?

MEGM is a major corporation; however, this negotiation is considered small at 800,000GC so their top negotiators will not be at the table unless they are there to coach an up and coming Business Development Manager (BDM).

Standard payment terms for MEGM is 30 days.

MEGM has been trying to grow their food bowl business as part of their 5-year sales plan to diversify products and increase profit margin for their cage business.

Currently, MEGM does not ship the food bowls and accessories, such as scoops and spoons, together.

What are the facts that only Martian Menagerie knows?

A new sales order has come in from one of Martian Menagerie's customers which increases the forecast of food bowls provided on the RFP by 15%. This sales order combined with a new 3-year agreement to be the sole provider of cages (including food bowls) for the Mars Military Juggernaut means that Martian Menagerie will now control 25% of the Martian cage market.

What are the facts known by both sides?

Both companies know the facts as stated in the RFP; however, it is also common knowledge, gleaned from customers and trade show interactions, that Martian Menagerie is not meeting delivery deadlines and that there are issues with the quality of the food bowls.

What are the Martian Menagerie assumptions?

Martian Menagerie assumes that MEGM has not heard about the new sales order or the exclusive cage deal with the Mars Military Juggernaut.

What are the adversary's assumptions?

MEGM assumes that nothing has changed on the forecast originally given on the RFP.

How can I leverage the facts and assumptions to negotiate the best deal?

The new sales order for cages is for only three different products; however, the majority of the order is for the Mini-Mars Button cage.

The RFP target cost savings was >8% but MEGM's quotation generated only an overall savings of 9% for the food bowls. If an additional negotiation for a reduction in price by 6% is gained for the Mini-Mars Button and the Mega Mars Marsupial food bowls and accessories, a savings of 12% will be gained overall.

2. Pre-Negotiation Planning

What are the goals of the negotiation?

Goal 1: Payment Terms

    Martian Menagerie – 60 days

Goal 2: Negotiate 6% drop in price for the Mini-Mars Button and the Mega Mars Marsupial food bowls

Goal 3: Bowls and accessories are currently shipped individually and Martian Menagerie would like them bundled and shipped as one item. Negotiate pricing for single replacement bowls and accessories.

Goal 4: The returned goods procedure is cumbersome and Martian Menagerie would like to work with MEGM to reduce the number of steps to initiate a pickup of the returned bowls.

At what point will this negotiation be considered successful?

The critical goal is to reduce costs, therefore, Goals 1 and 2 are the success criteria for this negotiation. All other goals can be tabled if necessary and worked on separately at a later date.

What are the talking points?

Cost Reductions (Goals 1 and 2)

Food bowl bundling (Goal 3)

Returned goods policy (Goal 4)

What should not be discussed?

Any product outside the Food Bowls and Accessories.

What is the fallback position?

Goal 1: 45 days or 2% discount if paid within 30 days

Goal 2: Price reductions no lower than 2% for the Mini-Mars Button and Mega Mars Marsupial food bowls

Goal 3: Minimum order commitment of the single replacement bowls and accessories to leverage quantity discounts.

Goal 4: Bundle and palletize returns to be sent back monthly or quarterly instead of the current timeframe of 10 days.

What is the walk away position?

If MEGM refuses to honor the pricing in their RFP response. All other positions can be negotiated.

Who will lead the negotiation?

Procurement RFP Team Leader

Who will be at the negotiation table?

No decision makers from Martian Menagerie will be at the negotiation table. All Procurement RFP team members will attend as well as a representative from Supply Chain including Delivery & QA.

What are their titles and roles?

Sr. Category Manager, Buyer, Supply Chain

Who will be the "Mystery Manager"?

Small Business Owner

What will be the tone and mood?

Upbeat but with everyone showing concern on the price of the two items being negotiated.

What are the trigger words for breaks and step backs?

Announcement by Procurement RFP Team Leader to run the current proposal by the Small Business Owner (Mystery Manager)

What is the setting & seating arrangements?

Conference room. White Board will have half erased "10%" under Vendor #1 and "6%" under Vendor #2 heading to give a subliminal message to MEGM.

Procurement RFP Team Leader will sit mid-way down the conference table and MEGM will sit directly opposite facing the white board.

What are the props?

Samples of the two bowls and accessories to be negotiated.

How do you think Steps 3 and 4 turned out? Did Martian Menagerie get what they wanted? Were their goals set too low or too high?

Each negotiation has its own flavor, vibe, timing, and resolution. This negotiation could have gone in a half dozen different directions. Be prepared, be flexible, and most importantly of all, do not be upset if you have to come back to the negotiation table whenever business needs change. RFPs generate long term relationships so be prepared to work with this company for at least three years. If there are too many red flags, step away. The RFP has already identified the supplier next in line willing to come to the table to work with you and help your business, and theirs, succeed.

This concludes the section on Negotiations. The contract is signed and now the Small Business owner has to figure out How To Work With A Large Corporation which, luckily, is the title of the next chapter.

HOW TO WORK WITH A LARGE CORPORATION

Once the Small Business is stable and looking towards rapid growth, it is only natural to set their sights on selling to a large publicly traded or private corporation. The relationship most Small Businesses have with a large corporation is a love/hate relationship. Love is when everything goes well and the profits pour in. Conversely, hate is when everything goes wrong and the Small Business is on the point of bankruptcy. Nobody can see into their crystal ball and predict the future; however, the Small Business can tilt the odds of success in their favor.

Since we've already conducted an RFP for the Food Bowls, we'll now focus on the winner of the RFP, Martian Materials Distribution, also known as MEGM. Martian Menagerie will work with MEGM to set up the processes and procedures that will govern the relationship and, in doing so, mitigate the risk inherent with working with a large corporation.

Signing the Contract

Be prepared to sign MEGM's contract template rather than the Small Business contract template. Note that all clauses will be biased in favor of MEGM; however, Procurement and Legal can mitigate some of these risks. A Small Business does not have the funds to sue if something goes wrong so understanding the risks before signing a large corporation contract template is essential to avoiding trouble. A few suggestions on mitigating risk:

- An easy fix is to make most clauses mutual rather than one sided.
- The contract should be read and understood by Procurement, Supply Chain, Legal and the Small Business owner before proceeding. Limitation of Liability, Indemnification and Warranties in particular should be carefully reviewed and negotiated.
- Make sure the Breach of Contract section is fully understood and communicated to the appropriate people. Avoiding trouble is half the battle in working with a large corporation.
- Focus particular attention on the Exhibits because these are the documents a Small Business will refer to most often.
- Make sure the obligations of the Small Business are communicated clearly to the appropriate employees.

Rules of Engagement

Once the contract is signed, it is the Category or Commodity Manager's responsibility to work with both parties to set up the "Rules of Engagement". Rules of Engagement is a military term for the set of rules followed by both combatants when interacting; however, it is a very appropriate description of how two companies start to work together once the ink is dry on the contract.

Step 1 – Account Setup

Account information for both companies needs to be input into the computer systems so that orders flow and payments are made.

A Vendor Information Sheet should be prepared by the Small Business to give to all new vendors. Martian Menagerie has received the following Vendor Information Sheet from MEGM:

VENDOR INFORMATION SHEET	
Vendor Setup Website: gww.MEGMvendors.mars	
Accounts Payable Inquiries	apinquiries@MEGM.mars
Accounts Receivable Inquiries	arinquiries@MEGM.mars
All other account inquiries	vendorinquiries@MEGM.mars
INVOICE INFORMATION	

Send INVOICES To:
    MEGM Invoices
    Martian Post Office
    BOX 387&4
    Grand Canal, Mars 389.L222L	

INVOICES must contain the following information:
    Company Name & Address
    Email Address & Phone Number
    Pay To Address
    Quotation/Sales Order Number
    Purchase Order Number
    Invoice Date Due
    Quantity
    Item #
    Description
    Price Each
    Sub-Total Price
    Shipping/Handling Fee (if applicable)
    Tax
    Total Price	

PAYMENT INFORMATION	

MEGM prefers all payments to be direct deposited by inter-galactic wire transfer at National Bank of Mars. If sending a check, send PAYMENTS to:
    MEGM LockBox
    Martian Post Office
    BOX 387&4LB
    Grand Canal, Mars 389.L222L	

PAYMENTS must contain the following information for each payment:
    Company Name & Address
    Email address and Phone Number
    Quotation/Sales Order Number
    Purchase Order Number
    Sub-Total
    Taxes
    Shipping
    Total	

MEGM GENERAL INFORMATION	
Galactic Tax ID	X136-387&4#0
Bank References	National Bank of Mars
	Martian Galactic Bank
	National Bank of Jupiter

The Small Business should have a new vendor setup process in place to ensure the new vendor is set up for sending and receiving orders, payments are made and received, the pricing is correctly loaded into the computer system, and the various departments are notified of the contractual obligations.

Let's talk a minute about...

WHY VENDOR RELATIONSHIPS FAIL

Everybody is happy! The contract is signed and everyone is celebrating because costs have been reduced and the balance sheet projections are looking rosy. Then reality hits: No orders are received; No payments are being made; No shipments are going out. Wait...an order has been received but the pricing is incorrect, the ship to address is wrong, and the order has terms and conditions in it that were never agreed to by the Small Business.

Failure of the Relationship between Buyer and Seller is almost always caused by a

****FAILURE TO COMMUNICATE****

The last step of a contract is not the signing of the contract but the communication of the obligations agreed to in the contract to the appropriate people within their organizations.

Step 2 – Vendor Relationships

The majority of products have been identified, negotiated and added to the contract as an exhibit. This product list and pricing must be input into the ordering system so that when the order is placed, the correct item number populates the corresponding item description and price on the purchase order.

It is the Buyer's responsibility to work with the Category or Commodity Manager to ensure the information in the computer system is correct. It is also the Buyer's responsibility to make sure invoices are paid correctly against the purchase order.

The Buyer is the front line in controlling costs and making sure the contractual obligations are met by both parties. The Category or Commodity Manager should be closely involved in this entire setup process, including checking the flow of orders and making sure the vendors are paid correctly and on time.

As the vendor relationship manager, the Category or Commodity Manager is responsible for resolving all issues between a vendor and the Small Business. Most of these issues will occur in the first three months so it is imperative that a close eye be kept on the processes initially set up between both companies.

A weekly or bi-weekly phone call should be set up with the vendor, Buyer and Category or Commodity Manager as well as any interested parties such as Finance, Supply Chain, Shipping, etc. to address any unresolved issues. Once orders and payments are flowing according to plan, then the weekly or bi-weekly phone calls can stop. A Quarterly Business Review (QBR) should be scheduled to make sure everything stays on track and, also, to identify new opportunities.

Step 3 – Vendor Meetings

A Quarterly Business Review (QBR) should be scheduled with large vendors by the Category or Commodity Manager to discuss the relationship at a high level. An agenda is prepared by the Category or Commodity Manager with input from Supply Chain, Legal, Finance and the vendor. Below is the agenda for the first QBR between Martian Menagerie and MEGM:

Martian Menagerie & MEGM

QBR AGENDA

- Spend Report
- Contract & Exhibits Review
- Inventory Report
- Returns Procedure
- Issues
    - Defective bowls
    - Missing scoops
    - Un-palletized returns
    - Outstanding credits
- Set date for next QBR

It is one thing to list out all the steps that *should* be done but there are some hard and fast rules that *must* be followed by the Small Business...no exceptions allowed. These are called the 10 Iron Clad Rules For Small Businesses.

10 IRON CLAD RULES FOR SMALL BUSINESSES

1) If it is not in the Contract, it doesn't exist
2) If it is not in the Contract Statement of Work (SOW), it doesn't exist
3) If it is not in the Contract Price Exhibit, it doesn't exist
4) If a Purchase Order (PO) is not issued, then the order doesn't exist
5) Verbal orders and email orders are not substitutes for a PO
6) Reject a PO if it is not correct
7) A Return Goods Authorization (RGA) label must be received before goods are returned
8) A PO number must be on all documents including the invoice, e-mail inquiries, RGA and Credit Memos
9) Payments must be received no later than 30 days after the invoice due date. If no payment is received, place the company on credit hold until the payment is received.
10) Do not waiver in the resolution to abide by the first 9 rules

10 IRON CLAD RULES FOR SMALL BUSINESSES NOTES

Let's look at these 10 Iron Clad Rules For Small Businesses one by one and discuss why these rules are so important.

1) *If it is not in the Contract, it doesn't exist*
2) *If it is not in the Contract Statement of Work (SOW), it doesn't exist*
3) *If it is not in the Contract Price Exhibit, it doesn't exist*

Rules 1), 2) and 3)

These three rules are specific to the contract. Remember the Financial Authority (FA) we spoke about in the Signing a Contract section? The only people authorized to commit the large corporation to a financial obligation, are the people with FA. Only people with FA can sign the Contract, Amendments and Addendums. Everyone else does not have FA authority so the Maverick at MEGM who tells you to just "do it" and "you'll be paid for the work" without a Purchase Order or Statement of Work to back up those statements, is feeding you a line of Martian doggie doo.

However, common sense must prevail. If the change is to add one or two items to a Product Price Exhibit, then wait until there are several price additions or changes before updating the Product Price Exhibit. Language for adding and deleting products without requiring an updated

Price List Exhibit should be written into the contract.

All Contracts and Exhibits should be reviewed during the QBR to see if they need to be updated. If products and prices have changes, an updated Pricing Exhibit should be prepared and signed.

If the change requested by the large corporation will immediately impact finances or risk then insist on an Amendment or Addendum to the Contract before accepting a purchase order.

4) **If a Purchase Order (PO) is not issued, then the order doesn't exist**
5) **Verbal orders and email orders are not substitutes for a PO**
6) **Reject a PO if it is not correct**

Rules 4), 5) and 6)

These three rules are specific to the Purchase Order and are very simple rules to follow.

ALL large corporations have a purchase order system. The Small Business invoice is paid against a purchase order. This is a two-way match. If the information does not match between the purchase order and invoice (allowing for a 10% to 15% price variance) then **<u>the invoice will not be paid</u>**.

Some large corporations have a three-way match between purchase order, receipt of goods or services, and invoice. If the Small Business invoice does not have a three-way match between PO, Receipt of Goods or Services and the invoice, then **the invoice will not be paid***.*

The three-way match risk can be mitigated by:

a) Always get Proof of Delivery when delivering goods

b) When working under a Statement of Work, always get a signature stating the project has been completed to their satisfaction

c) Reject a PO if the information is not correct

Building this simple goods and services receipt procedure into the Small Business vendor management process will save numerous headaches later on. It also create an audit trail for deliveries and service which is essential information for the Small Business A/R person chasing missing payments.

7) *A Return Goods Authorization (RGA) label must be received before goods are returned*

All large corporations are process driven and everything must be accounted for in their computer system. An RGA sets up the Small Business to be credited for the returned goods. Make sure the RGA references the original PO or Sales Order.

8) PO number must be on all documents including the invoice, e-mail inquiries, RGA and Credit Memos

The Small Business pretty much knows what's going on because...it's a SMALL business. This probably means someone speaks with "Max" or "Felicia" about the orders, returns, invoices, etc. In a large corporation, the invoice, email inquiry, RGA or Credit Memo is just one of thousands or tens of thousands of pieces of information flowing through the organization. Don't get lost in the large corporation labyrinth. Use the PO number as the compass for navigating through the large corporation's computer system and while speaking with myriad employees as the Small Business employee chases the past due payment. Also, beware the Maverick making up a PO number out of thin air. Validate the PO number with the large corporation if necessary.

9) Payments must be received no later than 30 days past the payment due date of the invoice. If the payment has not been received, the Small Business may have to place the company on credit hold until the payment is received.

<u>*The Small Business is not a bank or credit line for a large corporation.*</u>

If payments are not getting through and phone calls, emails, and requests for payment from the

Accounts Payable department are not getting any results, contact the Category or Commodity Manager to enlist their help. If this does not produce results, then place the large corporation on credit hold. "Credit Hold" is a polite way of saying that no goods will be delivered or services rendered until the past due invoices have been paid. Read and understand the Breach of Contract clauses in the Master Agreement and initiate if necessary. A letter to the legal counsel at the large corporation will produce results if the Small Business sends a notice of Breach of Contract. Be warned! The Small Business may lose the account if the large corporation is placed on credit hold; however since the Small Business isn't being paid, it is no great loss. Continue to work with the customers that pay their invoices on time and treat them well because their payments are the lifeblood of the Small Business.

10) Do not waiver in the resolution to abide by the first 9 rules

CONCLUSION

In this book, Procurement and Strategic Sourcing have been defined, Policies and Processes were established, a Request For Proposal was outlined, and Reporting, Negotiations and How To Work With A Large Corporation were discussed. It is my sincere hope that this book has helped, in some small measure, the Entrepreneurs, the Start Ups and the Small Business owners to create discipline surrounding cost control and risk mitigation as they grow their business.

ABBREVIATIONS

BDM – Business Development Manager (Sales Person)

BOM – Bill Of Materials (Direct)

BU – Business Unit

CAP – Corrective Action Plan

CAPEX – Capital Expenditures

CMS – Contract Management System

CAP – Corrective Action Plan

CREDIT HOLD – A polite way of telling a large corporation that no goods or services will be delivered until past due invoices have been paid

DIRECT – All products (BOM) used to manufacture the goods sold to customers

FA – Financial Authority

GC – General Contractor

INDIRECT – All products and services that are not Direct products

LOB – Line of Business…see BU

MMC – Mars Menagerie Company

OEM – Original Equipment Manufacturer

OPEX – Operating Expenditures

PARETO – Identifier of the 80/20 rule

PO – Purchase Order

QBR – Quarterly Business Review

RFP – Request for Proposal

RFQ – Request for Quotation

RGA – Returned Goods Authorization

SME – Subject Matter Expert

SOW – Statement of Work

ABOUT THE AUTHOR

It seems like just yesterday that I wrote, by hand, my first Purchase Order and entered inventory counts into a green ruled ledger. Twenty years have gone by so fast! I think Procurement is the most fun job in the world but most people will say Procurement is boring…just ask my family! However, there is nothing like the satisfaction gained from negotiating a good deal and improving the bottom line of the company. Everybody wins when costs are kept under control, risk is reduced, and the flow of goods and money move smoothly between vendors and customers.

I hope you did not find this book too boring. Pick it up, put it down, use it as a reference or, if you're desperate, use it to start a fire (unless you're reading an e-book). I hope this book helps you in your journey to become a successful Small Business.

Good Luck!

www.ingramcontent.com/pod-product-compliance
Lightning Source LLC
Chambersburg PA
CBHW070255190526
45169CB00001B/419